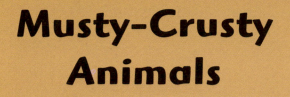

Musty-Crusty Animals

Barnacles

Lola M. Schaefer

Heinemann Library

Chicago, Illinois

Customer Service 888-454-2279
Visit our website at www.heinemannlibrary.com

Designed by Sue Emerson/Heinemann Library and Ginkgo Creative, Inc.
Printed and bound in the U.S.A. by Lake Book

06 05 04 03
10 9 8 7 6 5 4 3 2

Library of Congress Cataloging-in-Publication Data
Schaefer, Lola M., 1950-
    Barnacles / Lola Schaefer.
        p. cm. — (Musty-crusty animals)
Includes index.
Summary: A basic introduction to barnacles, discussing their physical characteristics, habitat, diet, and activities.
    ISBN 1-58810-512-1 (lib. bdg.)   ISBN 1-58810-721-3 (pbk. bdg.)
    1. Barnacles—Juvenile literature. [1. Barnacles.] I. Title.
    QL444.C58 S32 2002
    595.3'5—dc21

                                2001003280

Acknowledgments
The author and publishers are grateful to the following for permission to reproduce copyright material:
Title page, p. 7 Doug Perrine/Seapics.com; p. 4 E. R. Degginger/Color Pic, Inc.; p. 5 David B. Fleetham/Seapics.com; p. 6 Norman Tomalin/Bruce Coleman Inc.; pp. 8, 22 A. Maywald/Seapics.com; p. 9 Marilyn Kazmers/Seapics.com; pp. 10, 16, 21R Jeff Rotman Photography; p. 11 William S. Ormerod, Jr./Visuals Unlimited; p. 12 Rod Barbee; pp. 13, 19 Jay Ireland & Georgienne E. Bradley/Bradleyireland.com; p. 14R David Wrobel/Visuals Unlimited; p.15R Nicholas Devore/Bruce Coleman Inc.; p. 17 Stuart Westmorland/Corbis; p. 18 Peter Parks/iq3-d/Seapics.com; p. 20 Triarch/Visuals Unlimited; p. 21L John Cunningham/Visuals Unlimited

Cover photograph courtesy of William S. Ormerod, Jr./Visuals Unlimited

Every effort has been made to contact copyright holders of any material reproduced in this book. Any omissions will be rectified in subsequent printings if notice is given to the publisher.

Special thanks to our advisory panel for their help in the preparation of this book:

Eileen Day, Preschool Teacher
Chicago, IL

Paula Fischer, K–1 Teacher
Indianapolis, IN

Sandra Gilbert,
Library Media Specialist
Houston, TX

Angela Leeper,
Educational Consultant
North Carolina Department
of Public Instruction
Raleigh, NC

Pam McDonald, Reading Teacher
Winter Springs, FL

Melinda Murphy,
Library Media Specialist
Houston, TX

Helen Rosenberg, MLS
Chicago, IL

Anna Marie Varakin,
Reading Instructor
Western Maryland College

Special thanks to Dr. Randy Kochevar of the Monterey Bay Aquarium for his help in the preparation of this book.

Some words are shown in bold, **like this.**
You can find them in the picture glossary on page 23.

Contents

What Are Barnacles?

Barnacles are sea animals without bones.

They are **invertebrates**.

There are many kinds of barnacles.

Where Do Barnacles Live?

Barnacles live at or in the ocean.

They live where ocean water washes over them.

barnacles

Barnacles live on ships, **docks**, and rocks.

Some barnacles live on animals!

What Do Barnacles Look Like?

hard plates

Some barnacles look like tiny cones.

Barnacles can be white or red.

They can be gray or brown.

Do Barnacles Really Have Shells?

People call the outsides of barnacles "shells."

But the outsides of barnacles are hard **plates**.

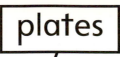

As barnacles grow, they make more plates.

The hard plates keep barnacles safe from birds and crabs.

What Do Barnacles Feel Like?

Barnacles feel crusty on the outside.

Their **plates** are hard like stone.

feeding legs

Their **feeding legs** feel hairy.

How Big
Are Barnacles?

Young barnacles are as big as the head of a pin.

Some adult barnacles are as round as large coins.

How Do Barnacles Move?

Young barnacles swim to a place to live.

They glue themselves to something hard.

Then, the barnacles start to grow **plates**.

When they have plates, barnacles never move.

What Do Barnacles Eat?

Barnacles eat tiny sea animals called **plankton**.

This picture makes the plankton look big.

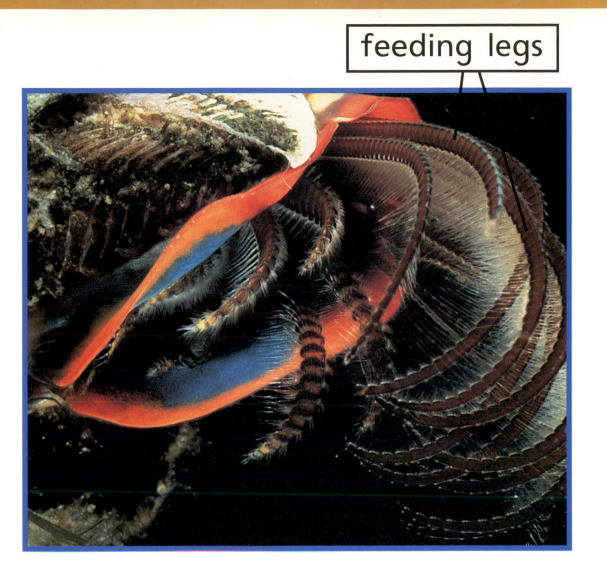

feeding legs

The barnacle's **feeding legs** take food from the water.

The legs bring food to the barnacle's mouth.

Where Do New Barnacles Come From?

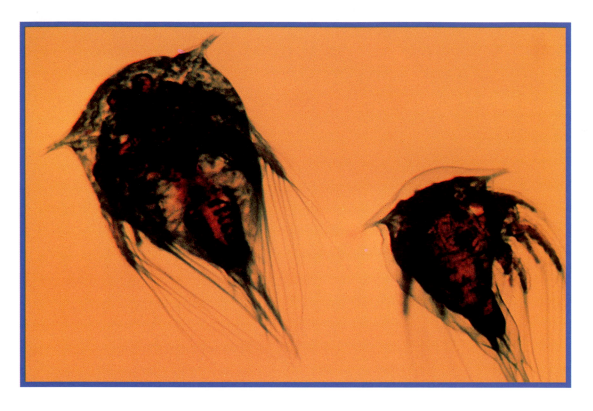

Barnacles lay eggs inside their shells.

Young barnacles come out of the eggs and swim away.

Young barnacles grow and change many times.

Quiz

What are these barnacle parts?

Can you find them in the book?

Look for the answers on page 24.

?   ?

Picture Glossary

dock
page 7

plankton
page 18

feeding legs
pages 13, 19

plate
pages 8, 10, 11, 12, 17

invertebrate
(in-VUR-tuh-brate)
page 4

Note to Parents and Teachers

Reading for information is an important part of a child's literacy development. Learning begins with a question about something. Help children think of themselves as investigators and researchers by encouraging their questions about the world around them. Each chapter in this book begins with a question. Read the question together. Look at the pictures. Talk about what you think the answer might be. Then read the text to find out if your predictions were correct. Think of other questions you could ask about the topic, and discuss where you might find the answers. Assist children in using the picture glossary and the index to practice new vocabulary and research skills.

 CAUTION: Remind children that it is not a good idea to handle wild animals. Children should wash their hands with soap and water after they touch any animal.

Index

Answers to quiz on page 22

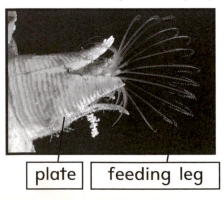

plate   feeding leg